dirty lovers

poetry and prose for the heart

Cole Goddard

What follows is presented as a work of fiction.

for anyone who has ever experienced

heartbreak or loss.

may you learn from it, and grow.

"The best way to get over a woman,

is to turn her into literature."

- Henry Miller

CONTENTS

ACKNOWLEDGMENTS

I'd like to start off by thanking my mom, whom without her unwavering belief in me I would never accomplish anything in this life. Thank you to the rest of my family for taking care of me through hard times. Thank you to Tyler, Kara, Mark, Josh, and Vince who stuck with me through the good and the bad. To all my other friends who held me through sad nights, or gave me advice on life that I may not have recognized, thank you. And lastly to the women that inspired this collection of poetry, I hope wherever you are, you're happy and healthy and live full lives with the ones you love.

a changed man

women,
they just have this power
over me.
it's true what they say,
the more I think I understand them
the less I understand them.
they're all so damn beautiful to me.
I've never met a woman I didn't fall in love with
for mere moments or vast entanglements of time.
and each one
no matter how brief
leaves me a changed man.

irony

irony,
fucking irony,
like poetry
reading between the lines.

I always wanted You
I would go to all the ends
of the earth to see You
smile again.

to hear your laugh or
see your eyes light up
as You share your passion
for the human psyche.

I was once your passion.

I haven't written about You
in quite some time,
and I hope to forget You soon.

it terrifies me that love
is this great massive feeling
and loss…

loss breaks even the strongest.

isn't it ironic that something
so magnificent as love
gets lost in mere moments?

fucking irony.

rebound

lightning

she was lightning in a storm.
she struck me hard and fast.
and when the dust had settled
my heart fused together as last.

before I could breathe
we found space in-between
the quiet moments together
addictive, like nicotine.

sometimes love at first sight
is really a love-blind darkness
a night with no moonlight
white on black, no starkness

what I thought were two hearts beating as one
forged in electricity of lust and cum.
the dust had settled, when all was done
my heart still bitter, my heart still numb.

adventure

belated nights and premature mornings
brought the adventure out of this hermit.
surviving off of caffeine like nicotine
addicts waiting for their next fix.

we found comfort in the chaos
a tornado through a small town
destruction on a short path
that's the trajectory of our chaos

it's another late night and I can't
keep checking my phone waiting
for your name on a hollow screen.
what are you doing to me?

i've always been an adventurous man
there's adventure under your skin
hiding somewhere between that spine
and rib cage cradled beneath your heart

it's a battle between the adventure out there
and the adventure in here.
as I glide my fingers across your chest
and your lips graze mine once more

yeah, I'll take the adventure in here for now

moments

this is my life passing me by
one moment at a time
to the pitter-patter of rain.

the phone rang and your name
appeared on the screen and
with a crumby joke I answered

"can't get enough of me, huh?"

laughter filled my ears like song
you just thanked me
for being me

darling that's all i've ever been

it's oxymoronic to find oneself
and it's even more pitiful to find
yourself through someone else.

yet in moments with you I shine
and in moments when you're not
here I am still a better man

shoreline

two worlds collide
every time sparks fly.
great galaxies
soaring through the cosmos.
our atoms aching to be closer
like fingers interlaced.

we yearned for more than we were
and the universe responded
in the most exceptional of ways.
we found comfort in each
other's laughs and bitterness.
harmony in each other's arms.
and safety in each other's heartbeats.

the first kiss had me nervous
like the rom-coms we make fun of.
but you kissed me true
and I pulled you closer.
we sucked each other's oxygen,
while we still could,
Jack and Rose
on a sinking ship.
water filling around us.
but we were never drowning,
we were finally learning to swim.

if my life is a sinking ship in a hurricane,
then you are an island and I am riding these waves
so that one day I can wash up on your shore.

little fires

you
lit a little fire
deep inside me
to be a better
version of myself.

not for you.

not for me.

but for us.

little moments

you're teaching me to find solace
in those little moments once again.
little moments where a cheeky look
follows a compliment and subtle smile.

comfort in the short stretches of time
when we are nothing but entangled
limbs and tongues
wrapped up in dirty sheets.

everything I could ever want
is in those sheets.
bathe me and feed me and
I would never leave.

the warmth of your arms,
the gentle smell of your hair,
the soft touches of your skin on mine.

so let us get lost in the these
subtle stretches of time
where cotton and skin become one.

a lesson learned in romantics,
warm light encapsulating these
little moments,
where time stops
and we find solace once again.

broken pieces

it's bullshit
to believe
that two
broken people
can create
something whole.

two broken plates
refuse to be
glued together like
the human souls
of damaged goods.

so why do we
believe that two people
who haven't healed can
heal each other?

when broken pieces will never
make anything whole ever again.

no matter how hard two lovers try.

space

"I just need space."

you can't change
someone's mind
once it's made up.
you can only let go
and hope that space
is all they need.

keep in mind
that space is
vast and cold
it's easy
to get lost
out there.

gallows

"thief!"

they screamed.
the noose slipped around my neck
and tightened, and tightened
and hugged me
like a lover hugs her man
goodbye for the last time.
she used to hug me like that.

the crowd gathered in droves
to watch a fool die
for his pirate ways.

to have loved and lost
should be punishment enough.

I accept this death
with all the courage
I can muster.
a lone man on the gallows
weighed down by failure.

they hang me for her pain.
my life for her broken heart.

I give my life to her now.
in this life and the next.

the floor drops out below my feet.
the noose tightens.
the crows will come for my eyes.
the worms will take what's left.
and I'll rot in hell for falling in love.

good at something

gods create canyons.
those crevices are the
distance between two hearts.
yet, here you are again
kicking the shit out of yourself
hoping you can
force enlightenment.

a tough workout
or another tattoo won't hide
the fact that you're suffering inside
they only help to mask
the heartache with physical pain
that's all you're good at.

but hey, at least you're
good at something?

hurricane

I was the water; I was the rain.
shrouded in happiness and pain.
you were the ocean; you were the sea.
now there's a hurricane inside of me.

atlas

this was never a story about Atlas.

I didn't shrug the world off my shoulders.
I didn't crumble under the immense weight.
but shit, did I come close.

I threw away her old writings today.
memories wasted in the space of my mind.
no longer a muse.
is that really what we've become?
is that what I've become?
dependent on a muse?

are we just two strangers destined
To pass by one another on the street
pretending like we don't know
each other anymore?

if it helps her cope, so be it.
I'll play the villain in her life's movie.
things are changing
and I'm growing to be okay
with each passing day.
I am nothing but a man
full of hopes and dreams
and desires and fears.
and I've learned
to step on the throat of fear
and remain in charge.
it's refreshing to stand
in the darkness
and welcome the demons
instead of hide away.
like there is no more

earth shattering weight
on my shoulders.

and someone needs to tell Atlas
it's okay to drop the world
because it's putting too much
unwarranted pressure on the rest of us.
he makes us look bad
when we can't handle
the weight of the world any longer.

but we continue to try.
I continue to try anyway.
strength is a virtue
much like patience
and persistence.
good thing I'm a patient man
and I must be persistent
because I haven't given up yet.
or maybe I'm just resilient.
either way, I'll continue
to hold the weight of the world
in hopes I get stronger
with each passing day
that we are strangers once more.

love note #1

I love how passionate you are
about the people you love and the
interests that you have. It has made
me own the things I am passionate
about more and it has propelled
me to seek out what makes me
glad to be alive.

finding friendship

three night stand

we made mistakes..
bodies entangled.
I used you.
you longed for me.
to this day, my only regret,
was giving you a taste
of what you wanted,
despite me knowing
where those actions
would lead.

jump. take flight.

I jumped in too hastily.
men tend to jump in before
recognizing the consequences
of what the loss of a love,
of a marriage, really means.
codependent tendencies
from another lifetime.
I just want normalcy
for once in my life.
how lovely it looks
from the outside, in.
two lovers enmeshed
In each other's arms.

loneliness rears its sinister face.
in the aftermath of these moments,
where I want to climb the highest building.
jump off and see if I take flight.

nothing left to write

I sometimes wish there was more to write,
but sometimes two people pass in the night.
and sometimes friends become strangers,
and that's okay because three nights
in something resembling paradise
creates a makeshift reality not worth living.

trust me paradise is a myth,
like the sweet nothing's
I whispered in your ear.

love note #2

I love your insanely captivating eyes.
sometimes when the light hits them
just right, you don't even seem real.
in your eyes I have found comfort
as well as butterflies. maybe
you're onto something as a green eye
supremacist. :)

on being reckless

guarded

she has the capability
to soften even
the hardest hearts
at a glance.

I think that's beautiful.

but she's guarding
her own heart
against the love
she receives.

and I find that
unbelievably sad
as well.

cliché

is it cliché
for this
white boy
to write
about your
deep brown eyes
that I continuously
get lost in?

half/whole

I wish I could
ignore feelings for you
like you do for me.

but I never want to
half-ass my whole heart.

I don't want to look back
and regret not trying harder.

I wish I could shift something
in your mind to do the same.

so I sit here in a complicated
state of existence where I'm
hesitant to go all in or
just go with the flow.

love note #3

I love the way your brain works…
and I'm not just spinning lyrics.
I adore your ability to think critically
and the way you are always yearning to learn more.
thank you for challenging my own
brain and letting me be the nerd that I am.

feeling lost

first date

'good thing I washed my sheets'

I thought
as we finished up our drinks
and headed to the bedroom
for a nightly romp, entombed
in the smell of your perfume,
forgotten time as I went down
on your sweet playroom.
we explored fresh skin
our sins loud and clear
like a romcom affair
a date, we weren't prepared
our fluids mixing to the sound
of 'I Love You Honeybear.'

ghosted

modern day relationships
are nothing but relation-shits
and we are puppets on strings
for all the world to see.

attached to those strings are nothing
but hollow souls and when they leave
they take with them everything
except the empty shells of
our once exuberant bodies.

you walked away without a word
and it took me far longer than
I care to admit, to get over my
ghosted texts to you.

love note #4

undoubtedly, one of the things I love most
about you is that you are consistent. you
always have been. each and every day you
make me feel loved. whether it be through
a morning text or evening phone call. your
love is a sure thing. that gives me the
most peace I've ever experienced and
grounds me. thank you for not making me
question where we stand, because you always
give us solid ground.

hookup

a one night stand in Colorado

a getaway.
a hotel room.
an afternoon sky
and enough coffee
to kill a rhino.
I sit here and ponder
the great machinations
of the universe and
ultimately what drives
every woman away from me.
would every path
lead to this moment?
I can't run from my problems.
and I sure as shit can't keep
living in a mindset where
the hole inside gets worse
every day.

I'm trying to heal,
and I'm trying to be stronger.
I'm trying to make time
for myself once again.
hallucinogenics and axe throwing.
wedding vows and donut cakes.
drunken shenanigans and botox lips
kissed this naked body
on a trip to Colorado to escape the
humdrum of life.

My mind was elsewhere, but for
a few hours I could forget that
there aren't enough women
in this world, to save me.

only I can save myself.

love note #5

I love the way you persist. when
your days get hard, you keep walking. you
don't avoid frustration or hardship. you just
keep walking despite them. you have inspired
me to work toward the same, but I can
confirm that it's no easy feat. you are
strong and I admire that strength.
I think we both know that is where
the lessons grow.

meaningless times

savages

like animals
we ravaged
each other
through and
through.

two savages
stripped bare
of all but
desire and lust.

where one
appendage ends
another begins
swallowed up
in the vestiges
of two dirty lovers
intertwined in the
living spaces of
forgotten homes.

the world
could end
in those
moments of
adulterated
ecstasy and
I wouldn't
even notice.

love note #6

today involves flat our appreciation for your
body. what it is capable of, all that it
has been through to bring you to the present
moment. how strong it has been and still is
for you. also, can we talk about how sexy
it is? your strong arms, strong legs, your
grizzly bear hairy chest. every piece of
you I long for. both emotionally and
physically. today, I'm just highlighting
my love for the latter, handsome.

the relationship

say my name, kiss me deep

my name on your tongue
is the sweetest flavor
when we kiss.
a nectar in the night.

say my name
kiss me deep

follow up

my name on your tongue
is the sweetest sound.

cliche I know,
but I can't help how I feel.

sometimes you'll follow up
my name with I love you
and I melt down when you say it.

celestial beings pt. I

gravitational energy
drawing two strangers together.
You, an inter-dimensional comfort
the world may never appreciate,
a work of art.

me, a piece of work.

somehow the universe
decided that our parts
made whole were finally
ready for someone to walk beside.

I'd travel the stars with you, darling
but first let us take our time
and see what can form
in the darkness of our beings.

favorite book

she asked me about my favorite book.
so I told her stories of knights saving
princesses from dragons
and armies of the dead.

I want to be treated like your favorite book.
the one you come back to again and again.
and each time you learn something new.
about me. about you.

don't loan me to others.
they won't treat me the same.
treasure me in your arms.
spine broken in, pages torn,
yet still forever cherished.

she told me to "treat her like my favorite book."
and I laid her down and opened her up, and
absorbed the knowledge her body had to share.

strong women

I'm not afraid to die.
I am terrified to live.
You took my hand and
along with it my heart
and filled something deep
inside I didn't know existed.

from the tips of the hair
on my skin, to the
cells in my bones,
I ached for a new
beginning with You.

as every other girl threw
themselves at my feet
I saw naught but
flesh and electricity.
just basic anatomy
created as playthings
for some malicious god.

but not You.
You were created to give
hope in times of despair.
as I rang the bell to your heart
You shook my entire
world off of its axis.

for to be a reflection
in your eyes is to live
a thousand lifetimes
knowing that in those
moments when I'm close
enough to kiss You,

our aching hearts are close
enough to beat together.

these words terrify
me to show You.
but show You I will.
because I will not live
my life a coward.
instead I will be brave
and give You my all.
a brave man at the feet
of a strong woman.

true beauty

very few things rival
the beauty of the mountains.
or the ocean's wrath and calmness.
or You.

always You.

but even the mountains
can't compete with your
face mere inches away from mine.

and the ocean has nothing
against the ebbs and flows
of my hand caressing your body.

as few things are truly as
beautiful as You.

breakaway

in the back of an Uber
You said,
"I would relive that day
 every day if I could."

and I smiled and thought,

"I would too.
I would relive every single day
if it meant it was with You."

then You asked me,
"is that a bit dramatic?"

and I smiled harder as You
rested your head on my
shoulder and I said,

"no."

hallway in a home

I was a hallway,
empty and alone.

and people came and went
not paying me any attention
as people often do.

they'd come to replace
my burnt out light.
or touch up the scratches
from years of neglect.

but she came in
innocent and gentle
letting her fingertips
caress my silhouette.
running them along the walls.
and she stayed.

calling me her home.

she makes me better

I thought
I would write
about skeletons
in the closet
and demons
clinging to my back
for the rest of my life.

yet somehow I find myself writing
about beauty and intellect-incarnate.

I thought I'd be alone indefinitely,
yet now those moments
alone aren't lonely,
they're just time in which
I can reflect and be better.

she tends to do that to me.
and she doesn't even realize it.

a head full of hair and a wicker chair

those long locks
flowed down your back,
You hunched over
your office desk
and me drifting in
and out of sleep
on your couch naked
like one of jack's french girls.

the sun set
in the distance
across the mountains
and the evening
slowly climbed into the room.

a scent of flowers
lingered in the air
as You continued
to ask me for advice
on how to write an email.

even while I type this
I remember this perfect moment.
our love seeping into the cushions
and clinging tighter to our hearts.

I came to again
from a comatose nap
to find you still at your desk.
in perfect harmony
with the street lamps
spilling into your apartment.

I watched You for long moments

until You realized I was awake
and You came and laid with me
until we fell back into round two.

the old man in the mountain

we sat at the top
of the edge of the world
and I held You close.
we gazed upon
the blue ridge mountains below us.
cities and entire lands spread out.
and our eyes settled
on grandfather mountain.
the nose jutted up towards the sky,
the brows sat in contemplation,
and the mouth held secrets
the world would never know.

and suddenly
it rose up out of its slumber.
a great behemoth
of stone and earth,
the golem stalked
across the mountains
and we watched it
destroy the cities we loved.
but we were together,
and that's all we cared about.

last meal

heartbreak hardens the heart.
I've no doubt about that.
but is that really
what this world needs?
more heartbreak?
more hardened souls,
numb to the world around them?

like a virus that strengthens
the immune system
love will strengthen our resolve.

so don't treat love
like an all you can eat buffet
for love deserves to be treated
like a last meal.

savoring every bite.

yellow

she went on singing
"but I wanted to die."

I wanted yellow flowers to
kiss her golden hair.
a reflection of the good inside her.
I wanted yellow singing and the sun.

this is true and it may seem strange,
that I wanted to be opened
and untangled and tossed away.

snort

I once heard an anecdote that goes
"fall in love with someone
you can get along with in the car."
as You laughed and
snorted under the luminescence
in my passenger seat
I fell in love.

your laughter
in the orange moonlight.
your kisses at the stoplight.
my heart bursts with love.

the dead

to caress your being
like a sailor appreciates the sea,
a fine subtle movement across a body
like yours, gentle and smooth.
humbled by your wrath, a hidden beauty,
and my god You are beautiful
in the way the Titanic splitting in two
was a sight to gaze upon.

I remember the two of us
intertwined in the drunkenness
of each other,
laying in bed for hours,
twisting and turning
in lustful entanglement
forgetting the dead
clawing at our bedroom door.

coincidence or fate

think about it...
if I had never
moved to Saint Louis
I may never have
moved to Charlotte.

if I had never
taken that job
at Lululemon
I may never have
become the man
I am today.

if I had never
gone to New York
I may never have
seen your story.

if I had never
tried to talk to You
we may be
complete strangers
today.

but I did try and
we do talk and
here You are
in front of me,
bringing me joy
and wonder
and beauty
and love,
every single day.

the entire course of our lives
could be different had we taken
a left
instead of a right
and I couldn't love
anyone else like I love You
because of the choices that I've made.

color my life in chaos

white,
sounds like cool air
in a tranquil soundless void.

purple,
tastes tart
followed closely
by the love of sweet.

black,
is cautionary pain on the
faces of animals in cages
too scared for their rescuers
who have come.

orange,
is the soft cloud like fuzz
on a warm afternoon
when the stress of life
becomes background noise.

green,
smells like the starving pores
of the leaves before
a heavy rain storm.

and brown,
is my hand running through
my lover's hair in bed
at one in the morning,
tangled in each other's
naked embrace.

smile

she told me
"your smile is a light"

but my love, if that is so
it's so, because of You

my smile is a simple
flashlight in the dark.

while your's,

your's is the sun.

the lonely mountain

let us
supercharge
the molecules in the
cold air, in this dark car,
parked at the top of this lovely
mountain and for an hour or so
this mountain is no longer lonely.

beautiful creature

the masked creature
in the white sheets.
a pretty girl with
the capabilities to sink
her teeth into the
fabrics of your reality.

golden skin
golden hair
white fangs

the moment captured
forever frozen in time.
a weekend spent with
the creature in the sheets.

clarity in us each time

I don't drive down
the lonely mountain
to get away from You.
I drive down so that
I get to see You again.

the drive down
the lonely mountain
is harder and
harder each time.

I just want to stay
with You up there
forever.
to leave You is to
leave my heart behind.

I don't know what I did
in this life to deserve You
but I'm willing to find some
sort of clarity in us each time.

movie like romance

I'll chase You across
the street in the pouring rain.
catch your arm
spin You around and
we'll stop traffic as we kiss.

because doesn't it feel good?
to take off your dress
and let somebody feel you
in the rain?

we'll never make it home.
instead we'll find ourselves lost
in the backseat of my car.

lost in time and space.

in the morning we'll
wake up with the sun
and your head on my chest.
a memory forever on repeat
like the movies of old.

you told me

You told me
that I am a sweet man.

the truth is dear
I am a greedy man,
and you are my currency

and like cartoonish gold,
You radiate heat and light.
I can always find You
in a crowd of people
from your glow.

morning texts

"You're lying
next to me
asleep,
and I just love
you so much, Cole."

as I get ready
at 5a.m. You look
so perfect wrapped
up in our sheets.
messy hair with
no cares
I smile as I put
on a brave front
for this cold world.

bon iver

your wet kiss on my cheek
forever imprinted to the
sound of Bon Iver.

your head rested on my shoulder
serenading the hopeless romantic
in me.

the flash on your phone didn't ruin
this perfect moment, it made
this moment perfect because I will
forever remember the imperfectness
of this perfect moment with You.

every moment is perfect with You.

divine beauty

I can't help
but curse the gods
for creating
such divine beauty
because if You
were to leave
I am sure
I'd never recuperate.

celestial beings pt. ii

two lovers in synchronicity
like celestial bodies
between the sheets.

capitulated to the madness
of sweat and saliva and
quantum entanglement
of what it means to be in love.

the aurora borealis shines for us,
the cosmos tells our story,
like the star machine
in our room glowing,
slowly rotating
I flip You over and
kiss your ear
and whisper
just how much
I love You.

held

if I could hold You
until the sadness washes away,
the world burns in our wake,
and everything is alright again;
then I'll hold You until it's
just You and I for all eternity
two cosmic beings exploring
space and time
in the confines of true love.

the wild inside of us

darling, there is a beast inside of me
a wyvern in the trees,
a kraken in the seas,
a dragon atop a mountain,
and a wolf sheltered from the storm.
I am the wild coming to claim back what's mine.

darling, there is beauty inside of You.
and I can't force the flower to see the bloom.
You must continue your path,
enjoy the journey;
because adventure
occurs in growth
not the destination.

and when you arrive
you may not recognize
your new self
but I will forever
recognize You.

unlike the flower
who doesn't recognize
the beauty after the seed.

with You

I want to write about You.
hell it is all I want to do.
when I'm not with You
it's all I think about.
pen to paper to pay
homage to your beauty.

I want to trace
the outlines of your body
when you're lying next to me.
but I doze off, letting
you watch me sleep,
into the early hours
of the morning.

and so I write
incessantly about You
hoping my words
reach You.

and maybe
you'll smile and realize
that although we're apart
you're not alone.
for my heart is with You.

safe keep

I want to be the one
person in this world who
knows You better than
You know yourself.

I'll never take control
over you.

I just want you to find
safety in that.
safety in me.

know that I will always
keep your heart safe.

archeological dig

I don't want
my fingers
to enter you
like a mad man
digging for gold;

but rather an
archeologist
taking his time,

slowly seducing
the sand off
the bone.

true north

she is my
true north,

true love,

southern charm.

5 a.m.

we lay in bed
toes touching,
You asleep and
I awake.

the storm outside
pounding on the glass,
wind howling and
lightning filling the room
woke me up.

This moment is perfection,
for my alarm won't stir
for another few hours.
I will lay here and enjoy
each passing second
with you gently snoring
beside me.

these moments are exceptional.
you will never know how much
I adore you in the quiet light.

the thunderstorm
cackling outside.
trying to draw us out
from the safety of our home.
the comfort of our bed.

a genie couldn't grant me
better moments than this.

honeymoon

is the honeymoon phase over
when two lovers
move out of synchronicity?
as they try to find balance again
one will go above and beyond,
one will draw away.
a push-pull attempt that
is the straw that breaks the
camel's back.
eventually the pendulum
swings the other way,
one lover
with hope in their heart
will wither away.
the other will
pick up the slack
but a pendulum never
stays in one place for long.
a perpetual swing back and forth,
back and forth,
back and forth,
until the two lovers become
two fighters in a cage match.
neither willing to concede
eventually growing apart
until there is nothing left.

I hope this never happens to us.
please don't let the honeymoon phase end.

writing instead of sleeping

it's late
and once again
I find myself
writing instead
of sleeping.

when I sleep
I dream of You
and me.
together.

some are memories
some are fantasies.

but there is one
constant in all of them.

You.

when I wake up
I am alone.

heartbreak rushes in
with such a fervor
that I am powerless
to control.

I wake up
with a heavy heart.
so heavy
that even
I grow weary
carrying it
around all day.

sad poetry

This is just another sad poem.
I can't deny I've needed this.

and so,
I read sad poetry when we fight.
it cuts me deeper than I can imagine.
a blade against my skin.

I read sad poetry when we fight.
someone else's pain puts
words to mine which I am
still trying to master.
perspective.

I read sad poetry when we fight.
i'm scared you will leave me
and the words could come alive.
demons that go bump in the night.

I read sad poetry when we fight.
and this time I am writing sad poetry.

what I want

I don't
want
your
attention.

I want
your
love.

currents

we must never
let the flow
of the crowd

move us

like the flow
of the ocean,
my love.

the girl in the bookstore

see her in the corner
with her nose in a book.
getting lost in the ideals
of great scholars, long
dead philosophers and
distinguished men and women
who have survived more
horrendous shit than I.

watch the sunlight pull
the gray from her hair and
the hazelnut glow in tandem
with her eyes, warms the room.
a Christmas fireplace with cocoa.
she won't notice you're
there, she won't notice
me anymore either.

but she's there, with
her nose in a book
about surviving the
Holocaust and she
will pull lessons from
it that will make her
a better woman.

and someday she will
be the best woman,
the best lover,
the best wife,
and maybe if you're
very lucky you will
get to see her become
the best mother.

but only if she wants to.

your side of the bed

i'm the type of man
who will sleep on your
side of the bed
when you're not here.

to feel a modicum of
closeness in the darkness
and distance between You
and I across this state.

I find myself sleeping alone
more and more.
and your side of the bed
smells like You
less and less.

take me back

I keep checking my phone
hoping, praying,
to a god I don't believe in,
a god You don't believe in.
thinking You will text me,
call me, FaceTime me,
anything to come back.
I would do anything to
hold You again,
kiss You again.

take me back to that first date
at the movies where I was
too scared to hold your hand.
to that second date where
I was too scared to invite you home
I was always too scared
of your rock solid foundation.

hell, take me back to that
Shroedinger's box moment
where the pause on the phone
elongates the final moments
that you were still mine.

how sad everything turns
in the after hours of a break-up.
tears shed, heartache pounds
and all I can think about is You.

It was only ever You.

senses

I still smell You on my sheets
no matter how many times I wash them.
I wake up and for a split second
I am back with you laughing in the dark
and then I remember you're gone
and the pain floods my chest again.

I still see You in every shadow and
every crevice, dancing in the kitchen
galloping around and doing anything
to put a smile on my face.

I still feel You in my empty arms
aching for You, wondering why
they no longer can hold You.
Pressed against me while we brush our teeth
the mirror showing our once perfect reflection.
now the reflection of a broken man.

I still hear your melodic voice
singing your favorite songs in the car.
holding me accountable for my shit,
asking me questions in the night,
telling me You will always love me.

I still taste You on my tongue
after long bouts between the sheets.

my senses are all but memories
of a love lost and a woman who
I would still do anything for.

meatsack

how strange
that one bag of bones
in a meatsack can love
another bag of bones
in a meatsack so hard.

I will love your bag of bones
until the end of my days.
until the sky falls on the earth
and the sun expands into oblivion.
I will love You until not even
our souls can exist
on the infinite planes of reality.

erudite

Chapman calls me an erudite
when she takes pictures of me
because I only like seeing myself
when I look far removed.

I can't help if the thoughts
in my head are too overwhelming.
never silenced.
always lonely but never alone.
so yeah, when You see
those photos of me and
I look as happy as can be
remind yourself that You
were on my mind,
always on my mind,
and there's emptiness in my heart,
because you're not here
in these pictures with me.

running away

thirty thousand feet in the air
chasing escape after escape.
will adventure fill the emptiness
inside of me that all these women can't?

when You left, I thought I had
nothing left to live for.
feeling like I'm six feet underground.
that was my mistake.
I had to create something
out of nothing.

so here I am manifesting
a life I could never hope to live.
from Miami to Minneapolis
New York to L.A.
and everywhere in-between;
I wonder if I'll find myself
once again as a stranger
in a new city,
or if I will always be a shell
of who I was with You.

the last goodbye

the sun went down yesterday
and refused to rise again.

your words echoing
in my brain
all night long.

"this is how I know I am making
the right decision. I love you but
you are not the person for me"

change

I watch the sky change color quicker
than You changed in those final days.
maybe You never changed at all
and it was I who refused to stay the same.

time has not been kind to me as
I spend hour upon waking hour
figuring out how we got to this place.

You left and I lay in our once safe bed,
wondering if there is a version of
us out there, that got everything right.

I am envious of those parallel dimensions
where we are still together.
You and I are no more, that's plain to see
but maybe out there we still remain unchanged.

what You deserve

You left me for another man.
I understand your reasonings why.
it took me a long while to come around
but around I have come. here I am.

and once upon a time I told You
all I cared about was that You were happy.
so who am I to stand in the way of that?

that's it. that's all.

a shot in the dark

the shower fogs around me.
It's not the steam from the shower
I realize but my eyes tearing up
as I break down again.

pain engulfs me
I collapse and the bathtub
begins to fill
Caamp serenades the flow
of tears like a waltz or a
country hoe down.

the psychedelics kicked in about
thirty minutes ago
colors vibrant, feelings taking
shape on their own.

this water is scalding
You'd be proud of me…
though I barely feel it
all I ever feel is the
emptiness inside me
emptiness that leads to pain.
fighting with the blackness of heartbreak.
numb then pain then numb again

I lay here in this hot bath
as hot as it will go.
steam rising out of the depth.
this was as hot as You liked it
I am burning up in misery
laying in a porcelain coffin.

tonight I texted You

to see if you'd like to have dinner
with me and this is what
I did instead

when You never responded
I knew it was a shot in the dark.

god's last call

someday we will get so high and
we'll shoot for the heavens but
we'll land among the stars
all in an attempt to get closer
to our god.
cause he's stopped
answering our calls.
and he stopped reading our letters.
and he moved away.
probably creating life somewhere
else when he saw what a waste
we've become.

and someday when the last rocket
ships blast off of a dying planet
I'll be left behind with the sinners,
Vagabonds, addicts and killers.
like a trash collecting CGI robot
searching for love I too will
search for You.
I'll do whatever it takes to get off
this planet in its final moments.
I'll learn to fly,
I'll learn to breathe in space,
and I'll spend the rest of my life
in search for that
everlasting feeling.

forever searching for Your kiss

before the sun rises
bringing a fire to the heavens.
before mothers kiss
the feet of their babies
and get lost in innocent giggles.
before fathers teach
their sons that being
a man is more about
nobility than notoriety.
before the rain and the sun
dance bringing new life
for the bees to serenade.
before the magic turns
to fireworks in the night sky.
before all is said and done.
I will whisper
I love You
one more time.

and after my words
leave my tongue,
my lips will
find Yours again.

I wanted to die

I wanted to die so badly tonight.

I didn't, but I wanted to.

and with that knowledge
I think I can stop writing
about You,
the what ifs,
the what could have beens.

tonight I feel a weight lifted off of me
I wanted to die
but I didn't.
and now
I want to move forward.

strangers

the realization comes
that we were always meant
to be strangers.

yet it was a privilege to love You
and a privilege to learn
how to let You go.

both played their part
in creating the person I am
today.

love note #7

I love your witty (at times) extremely distasteful humor. I finally have someone who knows the dark side and can laugh about it. You make me laugh every single day (snort laugh indeed) and it makes life way more fun. Let's keep laughing way past our bedtime.

finding oneself

quarantine

the government told us
to stay inside
in the name of health.

so we found passion again
in books
and photography
and art
and fitness
and writing
and in the wake of our isolation
we rediscovered how to be
more human again.

and pollution dissipated,
and birds sung for freedom of fresh air
and dogs rejoiced for their humans
were with them always.

and we learned that our way of living
was really a way of dying.

we needed a change.

she loves me, she loves me not

she loves me. she loves me not.
she loves me. she loves me not.
she loves me. she loves me not.

a warrior's heart with a poet's soul.
tatted on my chest.
Zach seems to remind me often
that he's found his warrior-poet.

maybe it's true. maybe it's not.
maybe it's true. maybe it's not.
maybe it's true. maybe it's not.

the mountains will crumble.
the seas will dry up.
the air will turn to poison.
the vampires will feed on
the bodies all the same.

and all I can do is keep writing poetry
to keep myself from going insane.
for if I stop writing the world will
dissipate around me and I will
disappear into the aether.

I've never known a love like hers
and I've never known a loss like that.
so I must keep writing.

cheap flights

before I know it
5 A.M. came around
and I'm sitting in the waiting room
of a too dead airport
across from a couple who look
so damned happy.

that used to be us.

I'm envious of their ability
to get lost in each other
around a group of strangers.

and I am gaining peace
in my state of mind
but it is not the same
without hands interlaced through mine,
and a heart beating in rhythm
and oxygen being shared between us.
yes I suppose I am happy.

but fuck, I am lonely.

everything is everything

take note of this pain right here.
don't shy away from it.
don't cower away.
notice it.
sit with it.
dig into it.
pain isn't meant to scare you.
it's meant to teach you something.
what is this teaching you now?
like a warrior trains her body
you too must train your body
to sit in pain and discomfort.
and like a monk trains his mind,
you too must train your mind
to be stronger than the body.
a perpetual circle.
strengthen your mind
strengthen your resolve
strengthen your body.

everything is everything.

vices

can we recover the lost
pieces of our souls?
those chiseled away from all the
drinking and fighting and fucking?

is it digression to want
to lie in bed all day
with a lover turning
moments into memories?

or masochistic torture
to relive those moments
in this notebook when
she leaves for good?

if this drinking and fighting and fucking
won't get us closer to enlightenment
then I don't want to be holy.

just give me a purpose
and a practice with which to settle
my mind in unsettling times.

once more

our lovers left our bodies
like abandoned places
run down buildings
full of mold and memories
begging to be revitalized
once more

our lovers left us
but we still remain
empty shells of who
we once were.
suffocating in loneliness
once more.

sacred vessel

messy sheets under love making
because I love making toes curl
and hearing your breath sigh
hard enough
to set sail to this ship
release the pirate in me
the siren in you
we ransacked this bed and found
treasure inside each other
a small navy and millions
of little sailors storming
your sacred vessel.

protest

we riot in the streets
but find peace in the sheets.
black and white fists
replaced with black and white lips.
yin and yang a transmuted chimera
barricaded hearts, barricaded souls
broken levies as we climax together
like rioters and police in the streets

pain

I'm hurting.
I'm in pain.
but I am somehow different.
the difference is how
I choose to manage that pain.
I lost someone I truly cared about.
but don't pity the broken poet's soul.
don't worry about me.
because I would destroy the world
if it meant I could hold her again.
selfish.
I know.
so.
don't pity me.

I'm different now.
I'm not the sad little boy I once was.
the chip on my shoulder
no longer defines me.
and this pain
won't define me either.
for the first time in my life
I am proactively
dealing with heartbreak
the way a man should.
yes I am hurting.
but I won't let that cripple me
from living.

swallow my soul

into the darkest part
of your heart you shall go.
the harshest pain
will be all you'll ever know.
your voice,
swallowing my soul.

ménage á trios

we are a menagerie in our
menage á trios of constellations colliding.
great balls of fire exploding
into black holes
our black souls
nothing but black holes in the
long consumed and used up
crevices of our hearts.
two celestial beings
bringing creation and destruction
to worlds within worlds, ad infinitum.
the cosmos weeps every time
a dying star loses its glimmer,
sucking up whoever was weak enough
to get stuck in her orbit.

augustus

the cold steel between my lips.
this machine was made for this.

"you put the thing between your teeth,"
I hear a voice begin to say,

"but you don't give it the power to kill you."

fuck you augustus
I think as I pull
the gun out of my mouth.

fuck you.

dia de los muertos

I'll show up late
to my own funeral
and grab your tear stricken face
in my arms and kiss you gently
into the good night.

and we can dance with the dead
on our graves into the dark
with tears of joy on our faces
as we celebrate our lives
and the ones we leave behind.

death is not the end
for us my love,
it is just a new beginning
for us to explore
the universe together.

nostalgia novelty

I'm stuck between
a comfort for nostalgia
and longing for new experiences.

a tug-of-war between
the past and present.

yeah I miss her companionship.
I miss her so damn much.

but the universe
has me realizing
that this was
probably how it
was always
meant to be.

and as much as I wish
two lovers can become friends,
or find their way back to each other,
I just don't think it's possible.

too many intimate moments
to bastardize logical thinking.

roadtrip

I want to go on a road trip.
just you, me, the open road,
and a playlist made of our favorite songs.
the blue sky, the green fields,
the black roads and our beating hearts.
the windows down for that country air.
conversation will guide us
we'll talk about anything and everything.
so long as it's your voice I am listening to.
and we will sing,
my god will we sing and dance.
and we will make memories
we will never, ever forget.
road-tripping with just you and me.

metaphor for life

I've been doing
a lot of soul
searching lately,
and the truth is
the more I learn
about myself
the less I actually
understand.

I think that's a
terribly true
metaphor for life
as well.

confidence

I want you to walk through life
with the confidence
that you're
beautiful,
strong,
capable,
amazing,
just the way you are.

stand tall with the confidence
that you're already everything
that this world needs.

and if you can't,
because someone once
came along and made
you believe that you aren't
good enough,

then have the courage
to tell them

fuck you.

kindred spirits

someday our pets will
grow older than us.
will that make them wiser?
I sometimes can never tell.
Penny watches me
and I can see she understands
my pain but doesn't understand
how to help.
she cuddles me
with her whole body
pressed against mine.
I glide across her fur,
so soft between my fingertips.
Mags get's jealous,
the youngest still learning.
but she doesn't push
penny away for once.
she only tries to join the cuddle-puddle
her head on my shoulder.
she licks the tears
streaming down my face.

no maybe they don't understand
where my pain comes from
but they do see a
broken creature.
they want to tell me
I am not alone,
I feel so lonely.
but I am not alone.

more

I'm learning to do

more

with less.
less sleep

more coffee.
less love

more

self depreciation.

the cleansing storm

the storm bashes the window
outside begging to come in.
I watch as lightning flickers like a faulty
light in a dank basement.
it's 1:22am and I can't sleep
but what was I expecting?

I'd rather watch this
behemoth of a cell.

the destruction
that comes with a storm
is often followed with a cleansing.
and I feel that on the deepest level.
like storms and the sea
that are apart of me.

the expanse

each of us is an island
in the expanse
and sometimes someone comes along and
shakes our earth off its axis
and it leaves our soul cracked
like an island split in two.
there's gravitas to the pick me up
the way we shape ourselves afterwards.
but sometimes there's sadness
when the cracks don't mend.
and the pieces
don't find their way together again.

a poem for my friends who picked up the pieces

the truth is
we sometimes lose our friends
when we fall in love.
I don't think anyone
means to let that happen.
it just sort of does.

we fall so deeply
into someone,
we get consumed
love rearranges us.
and before we know it,
were drowning in the aether,
sexual aerosol of love

eventually that love turns to lava,
consumption turns to void,
Beast and Belle stop dancing
and Gaston gets the girl.
that lovable bear is all alone,
shattered and abused,
and sometimes some friends
stick around and pick up the pieces

and for the friends
who are still around
those bonds last forever.

a short poem about depression

the mind drinks from
the river of silence.

and the body suffers.

god damned misery

when you love, you feel invincible.
you could fight a hundred thousand
of history's greatest warriors and win.

you feel as if you can fly
like you just may take off
at any moment and never
come back down.

but when you are heart broken?
it feels like you're staring up
at a stormy sky and you're watching
lightning strike you in slow motion.

it just can't strike you fast enough.

you wait for that shock to come
to end all the pain you are feeling
but you only feel the most
mind numbing pain you can imagine.

love gives you hope
and heartbreak takes away
every joy you have ever known.

we set these
unrealistic expectations
in our minds to give
us a movie-like reality.

but when we grow up
we're cynical and jaded
we begin to think that we'd
be better off living a life of solitude.

nobody was ever changed by love
but heartbreak will break you down
make you colder and more callused
to the world around you.

it's your choice
on what you choose
to shape you.
build yourself back up?
or continue to wallow
in that god-damned misery.

heaven/hell

trying to make a
heaven out of a hell
when all my mind
wants to do
is make a
hell out of a heaven.

ten minutes or ten years

whether I've known someone
for ten minutes
or ten years
I always fall in love,
but I loved that woman
more than anything
this world could ever offer me.
more than I loved myself. A first.
so much so that I lost myself
completely inside of her.
and when she left
she took all of me with her.
I had to build myself from scratch.
it ruined my for a long time
for a lot of people.
and I am not sure I will ever
quite be the same again.
women have a tendency to do that to a man.
they can ruin him
for ten minutes or ten years.
and I don't think I want to be ruined ever again.

reasons for living

poetry
beauty
romance
love
all the reasons I wish
to stay alive.

the stars are just
incomprehensible masses
of gas burning for millions of years
billions of miles away.
if that doesn't make you feel insignificant…
and yet we are the stars incarnate.

what if you were smiling?
what if you were running into my arms?
they'll always be here for you.

it's been thirty years and I still don't
understand the human heart.
it may take me my entire life
to figure it out.

yet all we have is this day. today.
right now. a bullshit line that strikes
motivation into the hearts and minds
of the young and the brave.

we could die tomorrow.
that makes us human.
so let's be more human.
today.

the waves

there is a strange sense of serendipity
reading The Waves
while listening to the waves
kiss the shoreline letting the beach
know that the ocean will always be there.

the sun a great protector
while the moon encourages
the currents to pull.
I too wish to be a poet and a lover.
and like a lover in the sea I too
float through the day with nowhere
to be and nowhere to go.
and like said lover I let the waves
kiss me, calming my soul.

"and it becomes clear and simple
that I am not one and simple,
but complex and many."

so please take my hands in yours,
hold me close and comfort
my weary head,
and tell me that
I am doomed to
always cause repulsion
in those I love
that you will still hold me
forever.

what I write for

I'm aching to illuminate
my human experience.
in the wake of what feels
like earth shattering moments.
human moments where
I'm most vulnerable because
my heart aches and my body
is sore and in the confines
of my empty mind
are thoughts racing for all
that I wish I could change.

I once wrote for You
and only You.

I don't write for You.
I write for me.

ejaculated thoughts
mind-fucked on messy empty sheets.

never settle

I won't settle for someone
without passion in their eyes,
without history in their veins,
without pride in their smile.

you don't need plumper lips,
you don't need bigger tits,
you need to read better books
if you want my attention.
I will celebrate your wrinkles
with kisses and your grey
with puppy rubs
in the morning.

but I will never care
for someone who worries
more about themselves
than the problems of the world.
I don't want to settle.

she taught me that.

the only rational act

love is the only rational act.

once you learn how to die,
you learn how to live.

love each other
or perish.

un(hinge)d

modern romance has never sat right with me
give me good conversation and some live music
or a walk through the park with a bottle of wine.

instead we get serotonin spikes with a quick swipe
and a spike of alcohol creating liquid confidence.

monday talks might lead to a phone number
exchange
and before you know it wednesday is the first date,
spending all your money and time trying to feel
a little less alone.

wash, rinse, repeat.

and sure the date could lead to an endorphin rush
for a few minutes but it won't change the fact that
you're hiding the self loathing you feel deep down.

but that's okay

because dating doesn't have to be about finding the
one
sometimes it's about finding yourself.

but if this loneliness lingers through each one
of these dates you just might lose your damn mind.

unrealistic dreams

let's be unrealistic when it comes to love
let's never get lazy in living

let's be losers forever
wake up nose to nose in bed together
smell of coffee and the taste of laughter whenever
and we'll forget everyone and get lost in the sheets
stay here our whole lives, never skip a beat
a million pictures couldn't capture these memories

no, let us be dreamers when it comes to love
let us never get lazy
and drink from the passion of each other.

a love poem for a sunny morning

your head on my shoulder,
the warm sun beating down
on this too hot summer morning.

we share a cold coffee and
you cling onto my arm
I cling onto these moments.

my shirt has never
looked so good
on anyone else before.

the dogs play in the yard
your laugh brings life into me
and a painted smile fills my face.

the wind caresses the trees
the birds sing a gleeful tune for
you and I and we smile some more.

your the first person I have wanted
to write about in a very long time
and now I can't stop writing about you.

I know I fall hard and fast
but please let this be something real.
something tangible.

and not just another love poem
for a sunny morning.

the night I strummed for you in the warm glow

I clicked on a salt lamp
the warm glow painted shadows
across your naked body.
your red hair glowed in the flames
of my lust and desire.

I picked up the six string and
sang you songs you didn't know.
songs with meaning for this
moment with you.

vulnerability is a strange thing.
it can be brave and
dangerous at the same time.
once again I am taking risks
so I strummed and you cuddled up
with Penny and Mags.

I live for these
picture perfect moments,
like a pretty girl in my bed

I need to learn to not read into
every perfect moment.
that moments are just moments
and there isn't a meaning behind each one.

dirty lovers

your freckles dance in the morning light
as we dirty the sheets underneath us.

your lips always fit so perfectly
as your tongue coaxed mine out to play.

your deep brown eyes begged me to stay
each time I leave your warm embrace.

your body like a puzzle piece to mine
lays perfectly in mine all night long.

I didn't think I could find someone who
could fit so perfectly into the fabric of my life.

I know this has an expiration date on it.
this won't last, we won't last.

but, I'm afraid you've woven yourself into
my heart, like our legs and arms in our sheets.

just a couple of love struck or lust drunk…

dirty lovers.

coffee kisses

'your lips, the coffee on your breath in the early
morning.'

- her, when I asked about the best kiss of her
life.

our last day together

I can see expansive futures with her,
entire lives where we live
happily ever after
but right now,
she just sits across from me
at a table in a diner
on a weekday morning
and I am at peace to stare
into those eyes.
those beautiful dark brown eyes.
and her hair glows
in the morning light.

she can't decide what to eat,
I have decided that she's what I want.
and it scares me because she can't see
the futures that I see of us together.

not long ago we were laying in my bed
and these futures flooded my head
and I'd give anything
to stay comfortable
in what could be our bed.

books upon a shelf

we're all just books upon a shelf
some pass us by and others pick us up
books with covers to be judged
judge me not
I don't want to be just another book
that you don't pick up gathering dust
let me be used and abused
spine broken in, so that you know I was loved
pages yellowed to show the storm I've weathered
for all the times I've said I am the storm
let me prove it now
and maybe my ink has bled through
for the broken hearts that have found solace here
and the words are faded
for the wayward souls still finding home
let me become timeless in your hands
and you always come back to me for more

reminder

a reminder to myself
plastered on my
bathroom mirror
to love when you're ready
not when you're lonely.

if only I had followed
that advice every
other time.

was

I was so in love,
do You understand what I mean?
the kind of love that birds sing for.
the kind of love that helps flowers
bloom in the spring and snow fall
in the winter.
the kind of love that makes you want
to sing to the neighborhood at two a.m.
when the poets and the drunks and
the lonely and broken hearted will
throw bottles at your passion.

I was drunk in love and unlike the
lovebirds asleep in each others arms
at two a.m. I was singing Your name.
I sing it still.

I was so in love
and I still am,
but I have no one to love
anymore.

free falling

kill
the part
of yourself
that still wishes
to catch someone
after they walked away
while
    you
        were
            free
                falling.

looking for happiness in all the wrong places

I searched for happiness
in all the wrong places.

in people, in moments,
between the sheets.

I searched on the highest mountain's
and the most inviting seas.

I searched in them, and You, and her.
I failed to realize how blind I was.

happiness always seemed out of my reach.
yet she gave me hope in my time of need.

I was blind
because I never
searched in me.

stream of consciousness

I walk through the woods with
Aldous Huxley's *island* speaking
somber in my ears.
some nights call for the quiet,
tonight is not one of them.

Mags pulls me forward
with her excited pursuit
of exploration,
Penny can't walk fast enough.
i'm being pulled
in two different directions.

always in the middle.
always trying to find that balance.

inevitably my mind is rambling.
it yearns for a six string and
the meditative crash of waves.
for captured moments and the
nostalgic overflow of pen on paper.
for rosy cheeks and cold hands
warming up in pockets.

what I want

I want to fall in love
with the woman
of my dreams.
the one who will
make all this pain
worth it in the end.
I want to fall in love.

And I want to write words
that move planets inside
of lonely hearts.
And make people glad to be
where they are with whomever
they're there with.

and I want to grow old
in the arms that will become
more familiar than my own.
and know safety and comfort that
only the luckiest have ever known.

and I want to fall in love.

live

you're underestimating
what it means to be human

to feel the rain prattle
down your naked body.
to feel the sun engulf your skin.
to feel a touch of a lover's lips.
to smell coffee in the morning.
to love and be loved.
to see the world every day
through fresh eyes.

there are so many reasons
to stay alive.

don't waste this day.
don't waste this life.

love letter to myself

You survived, most importantly you survived
the confines of your mind when all else felt
like you couldn't make it. You persisted, you
built up a resilience against the darkness that
has held you back all this time. That darkness
has become your ally, it has shown you the
importance of the light.

It's not a simple journey, but it is the journey
that is important. The destination cannot
become anything tangible when you look
back at how far you've come. Sure, the
triumph of success is important, but looking
back you will only ever remember the
struggle. The lessons came in the middle.
Keep that in mind.

And remember, sometimes you have to let
people you love go, it's a harsh pill to swallow,
but sometimes even love isn't enough. That
doesn't mean you should ever stop loving,
love harder, express vulnerability and dare
greatly.

This is only the beginning for you. Remember
these lessons, you have survived one
hundred percent of the bad days before you
and you will survive many more. When things
get tough remember that, remember that you
will face some hard times again, but the hard
times breed hard people.

Don't let that hardness bastardize your love
for life however. It's okay to be tough, it's not

okay to be mean. Kindness is everything in this world, no matter what.

Love people, love life, love yourself.

Cole Goddard was born in Las Vegas but attributes Hudson, Wisconsin to his upbringing. He published his first collection of poetry in the spring of 2021, 'Dirty Lovers', the day before he turned 31. This collection of poetry and prose encapsulates all matters of the heart while paying homage to his favorite band. Cole Goddard writes about the real harshness in his journey from divorce to the uphill battle of loving oneself. He blends pop culture references to bring attention to the unbearable lightness of being. Cole currently lives in Charlotte, North Carolina with his two dogs, Penny and Magnolia.

Made in the USA
Monee, IL
16 March 2021